Let's Create with Paper

Let's Create
with Paper

DAVE KING, DAWN SIRETT, and ANGELA WILKES

DK

How to use this book

Let's Create with Paper is full of exciting projects for children to make at home – from colorful paper flowers to individual party invitations. Below are the points to look out for when using this book and a list of things to remember.

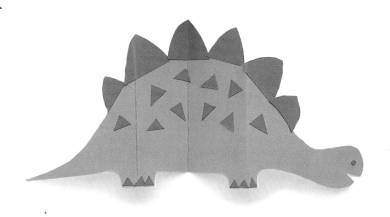

Equipment
Illustrated checklists show you which tools to have ready before you start each project.

The things you need
The items to collect for each project are clearly shown to help you check that you have everything you need.

Step-by-step
Step-by-step photographs and clear instructions tell you exactly what to do at each stage of a project.

Things to remember

- Read through all the instructions and gather together everything you will need before you begin a project.

- Put on an apron or an old shirt and roll up your sleeves before you start an activity.

- Lay down lots of newspaper to protect your work surface and the floor.

- Be very careful when using scissors or sharp knives. Do not use them unless an adult is there to help you.

- Always open the windows when using glaze* and ask an adult to clean the brush in mineral spirits for you.

- Put everything away when you have finished and clean up any mess.

We have used oil-based glaze for the projects in this book.

DK

A DK PUBLISHING BOOK

U.S. Editor Camela Decaire
Editor Fiona Campbell
Text Designer Caroline Potts
Managing Editor Jane Yorke
Managing Art Editor Chris Scollen
Production David Hyde
Photography Dave King

First American Edition, 1996
2 4 6 8 10 9 7 5 3 1

Published in the United States by
DK Publishing, Inc., 95 Madison Avenue,
New York, NY 10016
Visit us on the World Wide Web at http://www.dk.com

A CIP catalog record for this book is available from the Library of Congress.

ISBN 0-7894-1275-6

Color reproduction by Colourscan
Printed and bound in Italy by L.E.G.O.

CONTENTS

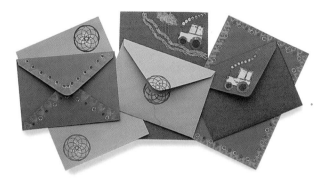

PERFECT PRINTS

Printing is a fun way to use paint and the results look great. Thick, sticky paint works best. All sorts of things, such as cardboard, vegetables, or even your fingers, can be used as printing tools. A sponge on an old cookie sheet makes a good printing pad. To avoid mixing colors, use one tool for each color and let the first color dry when printing one color over another. Try decorating writing paper and envelopes. You can also print on invitations, greeting cards, or postcards.

EQUIPMENT

Sharp knife

Scissors

Cookie sheet

Household sponges

Jar of water

You will need

Writing paper

Poster paints

Paintbrush

Printing tools

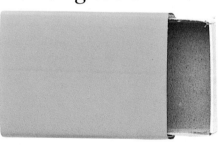

Large and small carrots

Small matchbox

Button

Envelopes

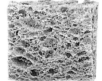

Cotton swab

A piece of thin household sponge

Plastic drinking straw

Large and small cardboard tubes

Thick cardboard

Corrugated cardboard

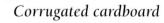

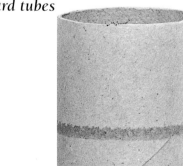

Printing the paper

1 Put some damp sponges on an old cookie sheet. Pour paint and a little water onto the sponges.* Spread out the paint with a brush.

2 Ask an adult to cut the carrots. Cut a sponge shape. Press each tool into paint and place it firmly on the paper to make a print.**

3 Print with different colors and tools to make a pattern or picture on the paper. Put more paint on each tool every few prints.

*The paint needs to be thick and sticky.

The finished prints

Try printing a border, a stamp mark, or a picture on the paper and envelopes. Make sure you leave space to write in!

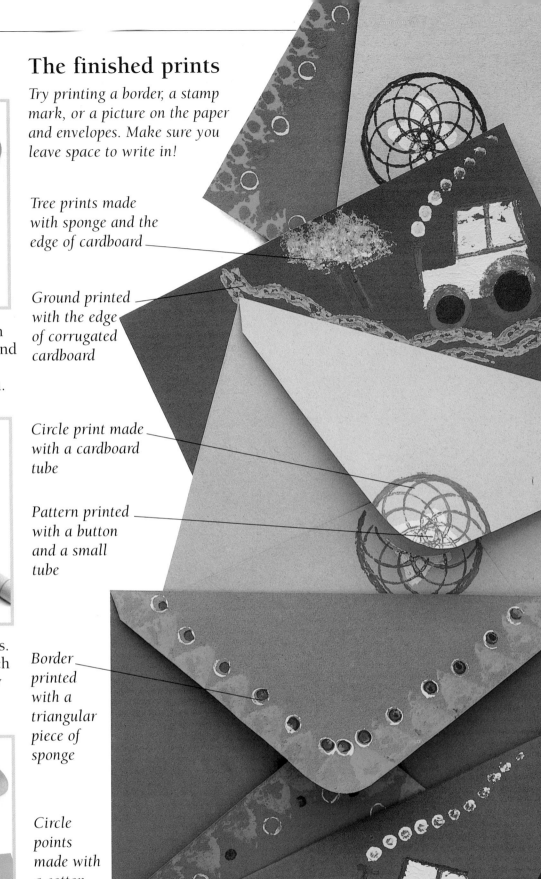

Tree prints made with sponge and the edge of cardboard

Ground printed with the edge of corrugated cardboard

Circle print made with a cardboard tube

Pattern printed with a button and a small tube

Border printed with a triangular piece of sponge

Circle points made with a cotton swab and a straw

Tractor printed with carrots, a matchbox, the edge of cardboard, and a cotton swab

**Practice on scrap paper first.

Paper Pottery

You can make wonderful decorative bowls and plates with papier-mâché (mashed-up paper). The bowls and plates are made in stages and take a while to dry, so allow two days to make them. Below you can see how to make papier-mâché plates. On the next two pages you can find out different ways to decorate them, and on pages 12 and 13 you can see the colorful results.

You will need

Wallpaper paste*

EQUIPMENT

Wooden spoon

Small bowl

Plates and bowls

Pastry brush

Knife

Scissors

What to do

1 Tear lots of sheets of newspaper into strips about 1 in (2 cm) wide. Then tear the strips into small, rectangular pieces of paper.

2 Spread petroleum jelly over the plate you are using as a mold.** (You will need to spread it on the outside of a bowl.)

3 Cover the plate with a layer of pieces of torn newspaper. Make the pieces of paper overlap each other so there are no empty spaces.

8   **Ask an adult to help you mix the paste.*   ***This keeps the papier-mâché from sticking to the mold.*

Petroleum jelly

Lots of newspaper

4 Brush wallpaper paste over the newspaper and cover it with another layer of newspaper. Leave this to dry for four to six hours.

5 Continue doing this until there are six dry layers of papier-mâché. Separate the plate and the papier-mâché with a knife.

6 Trim the edge of the papier-mâché plate with scissors. Paste newspaper on the bottom of the plate over the petroleum jelly.

9

Decorating Papier-Mâché

Once your papier-mâché plates and bowls are completely dry, you can decorate them. Here are three different ways to do it. If you paint the bowls and plates, or if you cover them in tissue paper, it is best to use bold colors, so the newspaper does not show through too much. You can decorate them to look like a matching set, or make each one different.

You will need

Papier-mâché bowls or plates

EQUIPMENT

Bowl

Pastry brush

Saucer

Jar of water

Paintbrush

Poster paints

Clear glaze

Pages from magazines

Wallpaper paste

Colored tissue paper

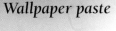

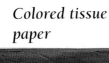

Painting the plates

1 Paint a pattern on your plate or bowl using thick poster paint. Paint light colors first and try not to let them run into each other.

2 When the paint is dry, brush a coat of clear glaze all over it to make it shine. Then let the glaze dry completely.

Patchwork plates

1 Tear brightly colored pages from magazines into strips about 1 in (2 cm) wide. Then tear each strip into smaller pieces of paper.

2 Paste the pieces of paper onto the plate or bowl so that they overlap a little. Let the paper dry, then glaze it.

Tissue-paper plates

1 Tear pieces of tissue paper into strips about 1 in (2 cm) wide. Then tear the strips into smaller rectangular pieces of paper.

2 Paste two layers of pieces of tissue paper onto the plate or bowl. Leave it to dry, then glaze it as shown above.

11

LOTS OF POTS

Here are the finished plates and bowls. The painted ones are all done in the same colors, which makes them look like a set even though they all have different patterns. The tissue-paper plates are covered in brightly colored tissue paper and the patchwork ones in a mosaic of magazine paper.

**TISSUE-PAPER PLATE
AND BOWL**

**PATCHWORK PLATE
AND BOWL**

12

PAINTED PLATES

PHOTO COLLAGE

Making a colorful collage using photographs of flowers and other natural objects is easy and lots of fun! Look in your garden, a window box, or a local park for plants to photograph.* For the background, photograph bright colors or interesting textures, such as the sky or a wall. Make sure you take several frames of the background photographs.

EQUIPMENT

Scissors

Pencil

Ruler

Prints for the background (We have used a rough plaster wall and the sky.)

You will need

Glue stick

Poster board

Making the collage

1 Cut white poster board to the size that you want to make your collage. Glue the background prints to the poster board.

2 Cut out the flowers and other objects that you want to use from your prints. Glue them down. Don't be afraid to overlap images.

3 Once you are happy with your collage, glue it onto colored poster board, creating a border about 1 in (2 cm) wide.

Check your camera's minimum focusing distance and stand as close to the objects as you can when you take the pictures.

14

The finished collage

Try using photographs of a variety of natural objects. We have used fruit, berries, vegetables, and a shell, as well as flowers. You could even add photographs of trees!

Photograph of a bottle

Photograph of the sky

Photographs of flowers, berries, and leaves

Leave a narrow border of white poster board.

The border of red frames the collage.

THE BACKGROUND

For a different background, try using photographs of a lawn, tree bark, or a table.

Photographs of fruit, a shell, and other natural objects

Photograph of a rough plaster wall

Different shapes, sizes, textures, and colors create an exciting picture.

Paper Flowers

Paper flowers bloom brightly all year round and make good Christmas or birthday presents. Arrange them in a vase without water or tie them together with ribbon to make a bouquet. Here and on the next two pages you can see how to make really lifelike roses, daffodils, and tulips. Once you can make these, try some others.

You will need

Clear glue in a tube with a fine nozzle

EQUIPMENT

Pencil

Scissors

Thread

Crepe paper

Cotton

Florist's wire

Thin wire

Making a rose

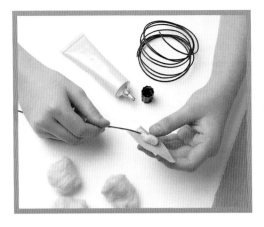

1 Cut a stem from florist's wire. Cover one end with a tiny piece of cotton. Wrap and glue some pink crepe paper around it.*

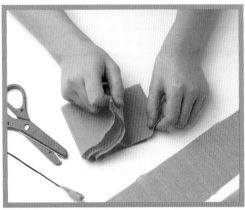

2 For the petals, cut a strip of pink crepe paper 31½ x 3 in (80 x 7.5 cm). Fold it in half lengthwise, then in half three times.

3 Cut the shape of a rounded petal top through all the layers of paper. When you open out the paper, you will have 16 petals.

Making leaves

4 Wind the petals around the top of the wire stem. You can fold over the tops of the inner petals to make them more roselike.

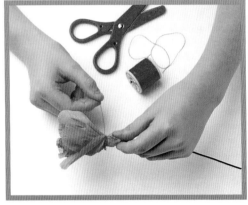

5 Tie thread around the base of the petals. Then make two rosebuds the same way, but half the size, to tie to the stem later.

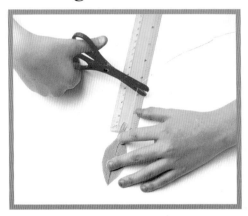

1 For each leaf, cut two leaf shapes out of green crepe paper. Cut a piece of thin wire about 2 in (5 cm) longer than the leaf.

2 Spread glue over one leaf shape. Lay the wire down the middle of it. Glue the second leaf on top to cover the wire.

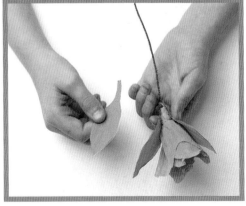

3 Place the four leaves around the rose one at a time. Wind each of the four wires around the stem to make them secure.

4 Wind a long strip of green paper around the rosebud stems and the main stem. Cover all of the stem, then glue the end down.

*All stems should be prepared in this way.

A PAPER GARDEN

Making a daffodil

 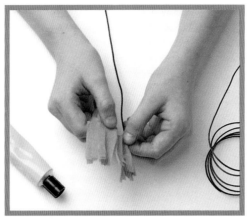 

1 For the center of the flower, cut a piece of orange paper 3½ x 3½ in (9 x 9 cm). Fold it in half and snip along the edges to fringe them.

2 Make a stem like the rose stem on the last page. Wind the orange center around the top of the stem and glue it in place.

3 Make white crepe-paper petals and long, thin green leaves. Assemble the flower in the same way as the rose on page 17.

Paper in bloom

And here are the finished flowers. You can make an attractive display using all three types of flowers or just one of them.

PINK ROSE

DAFFODIL

RED ROSE

Making a tulip

1 To make the center, cut four strips of black crepe paper. Twist them into loops and tie them to the top of a stem with thread.

2 Cut two small squares out of yellow paper. Make a hole in the middle of them and push them up the stem as far as the black loops.

3 Cut five petals 5 x 2½ in (12 x 6 cm) from red crepe paper. Tie them around the stem with thread. Finish the flower as before.*

TULIP

*See page 17.

MARBLING PAPER

Try making beautiful marbled papers and then use them to cover a folder. Marbling paper is a lot of fun. Special paints are dripped into water and form patterns on the surface. You then place paper on the water to pick up the paint. Marbling paints are usually sold as part of a kit. You may need to thicken the water with a special powder before you drip in the paint, so check the kit's instructions. You can also use oil paints. Ask an adult to thin the paints with mineral spirits and add a little vinegar to the water.

EQUIPMENT

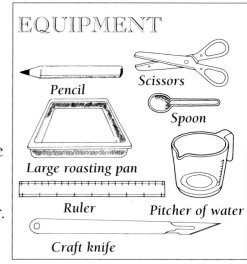

Pencil

Scissors

Spoon

Large roasting pan

Ruler

Pitcher of water

Craft knife

You will need

Ribbon

Two sheets of cardboard for the folder (¼ in / .5 cm smaller all around than the marbled paper)

White glue

Plastic drinking straws

Thickening powder*

Thick paper for inside of folder and flaps

Sheets of paper for marbling (These must be smaller than the roasting pan.)

Marbling paints

Strong, wide tape

*You may not need this: check the instructions with your kit.

Marbling the paper

1 Fill a large roasting pan with about 1 in (2 cm) of water.** Use straws to drip a few drops of each paint color into the water.

2 Gently swirl the paint around with a straw to make a pattern in the water. Burst any bubbles on the surface with the straw.

3 Lay a sheet of paper on the surface of the water, holding it by opposite ends. Gently press down on the paper as shown.

Making the folder

4 Lift up the paper and put it face-up on some newspaper to dry. If you used thickening powder, rinse the wet paper under water.

1 You will need two sheets of marbled paper to make a folder. Glue each sheet to cardboard to make the two sides of the folder.

2 Ask an adult to cut a small slit in both sides of the folder. Push a length of ribbon through each slit and glue it down as shown.

3 Tape the two outer corners on both sides of the folder. Then glue a sheet of thick paper to the inside of both sides of the folder.

If using thickening powder, stir it into the water and leave to thicken as instructed.

4 Line up the sides of the folder, leaving a small gap between them. Join them together with two strips of tape. Make three flaps.***

***Cut out and fold two flaps for the short edges of the folder and one for the long edge.

5 Glue the flaps inside the folder on the right-hand side. There should be a tiny space between the flaps so that they fold over easily.

MARBLED FOLDERS

Choose tape and ribbon for your folder in colors that will go with your marbled papers. You can make different patterns every time you marble a sheet of paper. Experiment by swirling the paint in different directions, or leave it unswirled. You can also cover notebooks or diaries with your papers, use them as wrapping paper or to make gift bags and gift tags, or simply frame them as pictures.

Strong, wide tape around corners

Ribbon

Strong, wide tape on spine of folder

MARBLING TIPS
• Make sure the paper you use is flat.
• Before you lay the paper on the water's surface, burst any bubbles in the water.
• Lightly rest your fingers on the paper when it is on the water to remove any remaining bubbles.
• You can make many sheets of marbled paper with the same water.

The two strips of tape joining the two sides of the folder together make a flexible spine.

The three flaps hold your paper or pictures in the folder.

Stick the flaps a little way in from the edge of the folder.

Thick paper is used to make the flaps.

23

PARTY INVITATIONS

If you're throwing a party, the first thing you need to do is make invitations. Homemade invitations are much more fun than store-bought ones, and you can make them fit the theme of your party. Here you'll see how to make three different kinds of invitations. Turn the page to see the finished products and to find out what to write on them.

Thin cardboard

Small sequins

You will need

EQUIPMENT

Scissors

Ruler

Pencil

Glitter

Glue stick

Colored ribbons

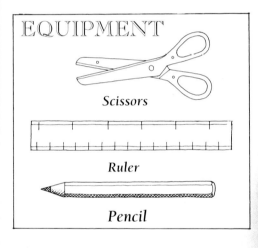
Colored paper

Colored foil

Cut-out invitations

Draw the shapes you want on thin cardboard, or copy the Easter egg or Christmas tree on pages 26 and 27. Cut the shapes out.

Christmas tree invitation

Glue colored foil onto the tree's pot. Spread glue over the tree and sprinkle green glitter on it. Glue sequins onto the glitter.

Easter egg invitation

Cut out strips of colored paper. Cut some strips into triangles. Copying the picture on page 27, glue the shapes to the egg.

Concertina invitation

1 Cut a piece of paper 20 x 3.5 in (50 x 8.5 cm). Make a fold 2.5 in (7 cm) from one end, then fold the paper every 2.5 in (7 cm).

2 Draw a figure of a person on the top fold of paper. Its feet and legs must go over the sides of the paper. Cut around the person.

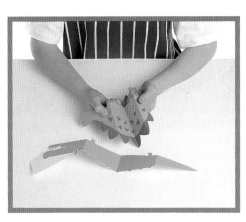

3 Open the paper out. You will have a row of people. Make a folded card. Glue the person at the end inside the card on the left side.

Animal invitation

1 Draw large animals or dinosaurs on poster board. You can copy the crocodile and dinosaur on pages 26 and 27.

2 Carefully cut scales, claws, and eyes out of colored paper. Glue them to the crocodile and dinosaur shapes.

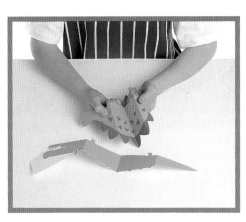

3 Cut out the animals. Fold each one in half, then in half again. There should be three folds down each card.

COME TO MY PARTY

And here are the finished invitations! Write the details of your party on the backs of the Christmas tree, Easter egg, and dinosaur invitations, and on the cards with the crocodile and the row of little people.

On each invitation write the name of the person you are inviting, then your name, the date and time of the party, and your address. If you want a reply to the invitation, write R.S.V.P.* at the bottom of it.

Colored paper scales

GLITTERING TREE

Make a hole in the top of each invitation and tie a narrow ribbon through it so that your friends can hang them from their Christmas tree at home.

Small sequins

Green glitter

Colored paper claws

GREEN CROCODILE

Shiny red foil

HOLDING HANDS INVITATION

Please come to Emma's party on May 4 at 3 p.m. at 3 Cedar Road R.S.V.P.

Concertina row of little people

Small card decorated with pieces of colored paper

STEGOSAURUS

EASTER EGG

Strips of colored paper

Triangles of colored paper

Ribbon tied in a bow for decoration

White poster board glued to jaws

Colored paper eye

To Sam

Eye made of colored paper

*This means "Please reply."

MAKING DECORATIONS

Decorating the room where you are going to have your party is lots of fun, especially if you ask some friends to help you. Arm yourself with a few packages of crepe and tissue paper and in no time at all, you can create rainbow-colored paper chains, giant streamers, and multicolored pompoms. Turn the page to see the dramatic results.

Crepe paper

You will need

Colored paper

Glue stick

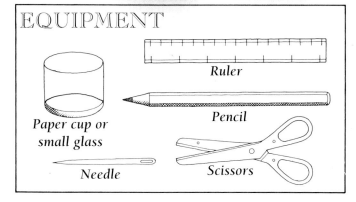

EQUIPMENT

Paper cup or small glass

Ruler

Pencil

Needle

Scissors

Thread (for the pompoms)

Tissue paper

Tape

Streamers

1 Cut two long strips of crepe paper the same width, keeping the paper folded. Snip along the edges of the strips to fringe them.

2 Tape the strips of paper together at one end. Twist them together all the way along. Tape the other ends together.

Rainbow chains

1 Cut colored paper or crepe paper into long strips about 1 in (2.5 cm) wide. For a rainbow chain, use lots of different colors.

2 Cut each strip into pieces about 7 in (18 cm) long. Roll a piece of paper into a ring, as shown, and glue down the outer edge.

3 Loop another piece of paper through the ring and glue it. Keep on doing this until the chain is the length you want.

Braided chain

1 Cut two long strips of different-colored crepe paper the same width.* Tape the two ends together, as shown here.

2 Fold the bottom strip of paper across the top strip. Then fold the new bottom strip of paper up over the strip of paper on top.

3 Keep braiding the two strips of paper together. Tape the ends together. Then gently pull the ends of the chain apart.

Tissue-paper pompoms

1 Draw circles on folded colored tissue paper by drawing around a paper cup or glass. Cut the circles out.

2 Fold eight circles of tissue paper into quarters. Sew the point of each one onto a knotted piece of thread.

3 Make two small stitches in the tissue paper and cut the thread, leaving a loose end. Open out each circle of paper.

*Leave the paper folded, as it is in the packet, when you cut it.

DASHING DECORATIONS

Tape the paper chains and streamers to the walls of your party room, or loop them around fireplaces, doorways, mirrors, and pictures (ask your parents first). Hang or tape groups of tissue-paper pompoms in the joins between two streamers or chains. Your room will be full of color, ready for the party to begin.

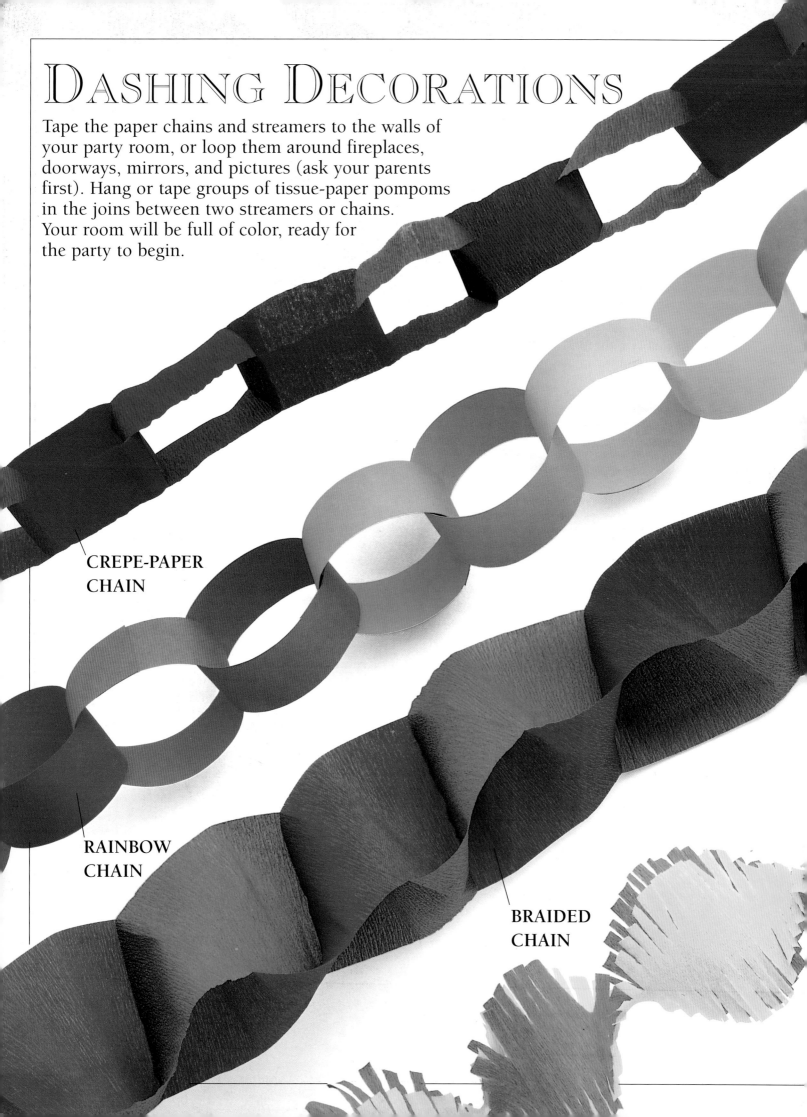

CREPE-PAPER CHAIN

RAINBOW CHAIN

BRAIDED CHAIN

CREPE-PAPER
STREAMER

TISSUE-PAPER
POMPOMS

31

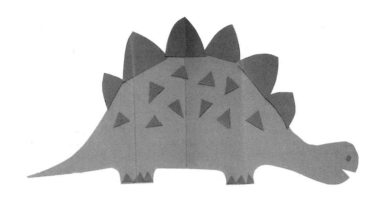